Disclaimer Notice:

Please note the information contained within this document is for educational and entertainment purposes only. All effort has been executed to present accurate, up to date, reliable, complete information. No warranties of any kind are declared or implied. Readers acknowledge that the author is not engaged in the rendering of legal, financial, medical, or professional advice. The content within this book has been derived from various sources. Please consult a licensed professional before attempting any techniques outlined in this book.

CONTENTS

Chapter 1- All you need to know about the low-carb diet

Dear readers, before I start the book, it is very important for you to understand what a low-carb diet is.

What Is Low-carb Diet?

A diet that restricts the carbohydrate intake and stresses on the intake of food that is rich in fats and proteins is called a low-carb diet. Carbs found in grains, fruits, or starchy veggies are kept off-limits.

For each diet, the restrictions vary according to the type and quantity of carbs you can eat. The daily carb allowance on a moderately low-carb diet is 20-50grams.

Rules of a low-carb diet

When you plan to go on a low-carb diet, consider following a few rules. These rules should not only be in your head, you need to apply them in a practical scenario. Please go through these rules one by one.

Your "fat friend": Know that healthy fats like foods rich in omega-3 fatty acids are going to be your best buddies in the low-carb journey.

Sugar is the sweet poison: Consider sugar as toxic. If your body is unable to process sugar in the right way, devastating health issues are bound to happen.

Don't be fooled by the low-carb label: foods labeled as "low-carb" are actually high in carb content.

Go green: Your meal should contain a considerable portion are greens. They are a great substitute for starch.

Chant the fat, fiber, and protein mantra: Your plate should be filled with these three nutrients as they fulfill the prerequisites of a low-carb diet.

Make few rules: Make few and simple rules that you can conveniently follow without overriding any.

Advantages of a low-carb diet

Below are a few scientifically backed health benefits of following a low-carb diet.

Low-carb diets automatically limit your appetite.

Low-carb diets led to quicker weight loss as compared to any other known form for dieting.

This diet helps you get rid of the abdominal fat.

Low-carb diets help in reducing the triglyceride levels that can cause damage to many viscera.

This diet increases the levels of the good cholesterol(HDL) in your blood.

Low-carb foods help to overcome Type 2 diabetes.

Reducing the carb intake results in a stable blood pressure.

Low-carb diets are the best-suited treatment for the metabolic syndrome.
A low-carb diet is considered as a therapy for several brain-related malfunctions like epilepsy, Alzheimer's disease, and Parkinson's disease.

Some Symptoms to Recognize

Switching over from glucose to fats as the primary energy source is a large scale metabolic change.
Your body doesn't easily accept it and it communicates about the alteration to you through various symptoms. The symptoms vary from person to person and usually last for a week or more.
Here are a few symptoms you should be aware of.
Nausea
Vomiting
A headache
Restlessness
Carb-cravings
Bad breath
Diarrhea
Mood swings
Dizziness
Muscle cramps
Lack of focus
Stomach cramps
Insomnia
Sore muscles
Don't be distressed. The symptoms will soon disappear.

Useful Tips on Successful Low-carb Diet Journey

Following a low-carb diet is a tricky affair, especially if you a first-time dieter. Below are a few quick tips.
Keep yourself updated about all the low-carb and high-fat food choices.
Keep a track of the carb count of each food that you include in your menu.
Draft a diet plan and make sure you stick to it.
Preparing meals proactively is a great practice.
Keep low-carb snacks handy to munch whenever you feel like.
Carbs are the nice guys and evil ones too. Refined sugar is the evil one while carb in veggies is good for you. Make sure you befriend the right one and keep the evil ones off limits.
Replace high-carb food with a low-carb option and reap the benefits.
Spend some time in the gym. Perform some light workouts. Don't go on any extreme though.

Update yourself about the side effects of carb withdrawal. You may experience a few.

What to Prepare before Diving into the Low-carb Diet?

Stuffing your fridge with the right kinds of food and being head-strong are the two prerequisites of a low-carb diet.

Go through the simple step-by-step guide given below. It will be of some help.

1. Be clear about the foods that you can consume and the food you can't.
2. Make fat your best friend. Get over your fat phobia.
3. Spend some time in the kitchen and polish your cooking skills.
4. Be prepared to face the symptoms of carb withdrawal.
5. Upsurge your electrolyte intake. Make sure you get plenty of sodium and potassium.

Common Mistakes to Avoid

Your whole effort of following a low-carb diet can be rendered worthless if you fail to identify and avoid some common mistakes.

Have a quick look.

Not keeping a track of your macros.

Eating inadequate fats and proteins.

Not consuming enough fiber and green leafy veggies.

Not getting enough sleep.

Munching too many nuts.

Eating a lot of low-carb food that results in overriding the daily carb allowance.

Following the "low-carb label" blindly.

Not drafting a plan proactively.

Not exercising regularly.

Having regular cheat meals.

Suffering from some health conditions like diabetes, hypertension, and hypothyroidism.

Being dehydrated and taking fewer electrolytes.

FAQs of Low-carb Diet Program

Please go through a few FAQs that usually arise when you decide to take up a low-carb diet.

Q: Is it important to calculate the calories of each diet?

A: No. Low-carb diet naturally decreases your capacity to eat. Thus, you don't need to count your daily calories.

Q: Is tracking macros important?

A: Yes. You should be well aware of your protein, fat, and carb intake.

Q: Should I eat something in every three hours?

A: Eat when you feel like. Neither wait for the hunger to grow nor eat every now and then.

Q: I have a sweet tooth. What to do?

A: Use some Stevia, monk fruit, or erythritol. These are good quality sugar substitutes.

Q: How will I fight the symptoms of a low-carb diet?

A: Drink plenty of water, stay stress-free, sleep well, and relax.

By now, you are well introduced to what a low-carb diet is all about. In the coming chapter, I will give you some shopping tips for a low-carb diet.

Chapter 2: Low-carb Diet Shopping Guide

So, you have planned to follow a low-carb diet and you hit the nearby grocery store to do some shopping. The moment you step into the store, you see the shelves packed with literally hundreds of food choices. You feel lost and confused. What should I buy and what should I avoid?

Well, you can easily overcome this "not so funny" situation by preparing your shopping list in advance and knowing which foods are low-carb, high-fat, and adequate in proteins.

This will save a lot of energy, money, and time at the.

I have provided a shopping list guide that can you follow. Please have a look.

What to Eat

One simple advice. Leave what tastes sweet. Here is a guide on the veggies, meat, fruits, and dairy you should buy. Have a look.

Vegetables: consume plenty of these veggies. These low-carb veggies are extremely beneficial for your health and rich in nutrition.

Artichokes	Chives	Lettuce	Shallots
Asparagus	Cucumber	Mushrooms	Sea veggies
Broccoli	Eggplant	Okra	Spinach
Sprouts	Fennel	Onions	Tomatoes
Butterhead Lettuce	Garlic	Parsley	Zucchini
Cabbage	Kale	Pumpkin	
Cauliflower	Leeks	Radish	
Celery	Leafy Greens	Scallions	

Fermented Vegetables

Kimchi	Sauerkraut

Fruits: you are not allowed to have most of the fruits as fruits are naturally rich in carb content. However, there are a few citrus fruits that you should consume.

Avocado	Lemon	Strawberry
Blackberry	Lime	Guava
Blueberry	Olive	Papaya
Cranberry	Raspberry	Citrus orange

Meat: meat is a part and parcel of a low-carb meal. Make sure you buy the fatty cuts to increase your fat and protein intake.

Beef	Duck	Pork
Bison	Goat	Reindeer

Chicken	Goose	Sheep
Deer	Lamb	Turkey

Processed meat(carb-free)

Sausage	Salami
Hot dogs	Bacon
Pepperoni	

Organ meat

Bone marrow	Liver
Heart	Tongue
Kidney	Brain

Legumes: most of the legumes are carb-rich. So, they are off limits. However, you can consume the following.

Green beans	Peas

Fats: Fats are extremely important for a low-carb diet provided you select the right kind of fat from the right source. Here is a list of a few healthy fats.

Avocado oil	Ghee	Red palm oil
Cocoa butter	Lard	Sesame oil
Coconut oil	MCT oil	Tallow
Duck fat	Olive oil	Walnut oil

Fish: There is no other known source of Omega-3 fatty acids as good as fish. Consume a portion of fish in every alternate meal if you can.

Bass	Haddock	Mackerel
Cod	Halibut	Perch
Eel	Herring	Red snapper
Rockfish	Salmon	Sardines
Tuna	Turbot	Trout

Other seafood:All seafood is highly nutritious with little carb. Buy the following if your pocket allows.

Abalone	Oysters
Clams	Shrimp
Crab	Squid
Lobster	

Nuts and seeds: nuts and seeds are high in fats and low in carbs. Munch a few when you want to. Keep a check because overeating nuts are easy, and you don't even realize.

Almonds	Sesame seeds	Nut butter
Hazelnuts	Sunflower seeds	Hemp seeds
Pecans	Walnuts	

Pistachios	Cashews
Pumpkin seeds	Chia seeds

Herbs and spices: for cooking your low-carb meals, consider using the following spices.

Sea salt	Chili powder	Rosemary	Cinnamon
Black pepper	Cayenne powder	Sage	Nutmeg
White pepper	Cumin	Turmeric	Cloves
Basil	Oregano	Parsley	Ginger
Italian seasoning	Thyme	Cilantro	Cardamom
Paprika	Dill		

Dairy: dairy fulfills a low-carb meal because of its high-fat and low-carb content. Buy the following in bulk.

Ghee	Eggs	Cheese

Other foods you should eat: these are the other food items that can be a part of your low-carb menu.

Homemade condiments	Cod liver oil	Mustard	Tamari sauce
Coconut butter	Unsweetened cocoa powder	Hot sauce	Coconut aminos
Beef jerky	Vinegar	Vanilla extract	Fish sauce
Pickles	Shredded coconut	Coconut flour	Gelatin
100% dark chocolate	Stevia	Monk fruit	Almond flour

What to Avoid

A low-carb diet won't work if you are not well aware of what to avoid as much as you are aware of what to eat. There are literally hundreds of things out there that are the known enemies of a low-carb diet. Make sure you don't purchase any of these. Have a look.

Sugars:Sugar is the sweet poison of a low-carb diet. It is strictly banned in any form whatsoever.

White sugar	Honey	Agave
Fructose	Glucose	Coconut sugar
Corn syrup	Maple syrup	Brown sugar
Dextrose	Maltose	Lactose

Grains: grains are high in carb content and not allowed in a low-carb diet.

Wheat	Couscous	Oats	Rice flour

White flour	All-purpose flour	Barley	Millet
Quinoa	Rice	Cornmeal	Bran
Rye	Wheat flour	Corn	Buckwheat

Processed foods: Processed food in any form should be avoided. Though these are labeled as "low-carb" but it is a known secret that these actually contain high carb content.

Bread	Candy	Pancakes	Baked goods
Potato chips	Crackers	Ketchup	Snack bars
Ice cream	Tortilla chips	Dressing	Cereal
Waffles	Pretzels	Cookies	Most sauces

Fruits: Fruits are sweet and rich in carbs. Though you may be fond of these, on a low-carb diet, avoid the following.

Canned fruits	Pomegranate	Kiwi	Apricot
Apples	Nectarines	Dates	Papaya
Sweet oranges	Grapes	Bananas	Fig
Pears	Watermelon	Cherries	
Peaches	Cantaloupe	Mango	

Legumes: here are the legumes that you should not purchase due to their high-carb content.

All beans	Lentils	Soybeans

Low-carb foods: A low-carb food doesn't mean it can be a part of the low-carb meal. Avoid these as much as you can.

Sugar alcohols	Artificial sweeteners	Peanut butter
Cheese salad dressing	Low-carb gluten-containing products	Diet Sodas

Advice of Drink

I have dedicated a separate section on drinks because drinks are known to be mischievous as far as hidden carb content is concerned. Though most of the drinks are thought to be carb-free, the scenario is not always true. I highly recommend you to look for the nutritional information of a drink before gulping it.

Drinks you should have:Buy the following drinks provided you pick up the unsweetened cane.

Almond milk	Coconut milk	Sparkling mineral water
Cashew milk	Unsweetened coffee	Sweetened tea

Broth	Herbal teas	Water
Club soda	Seltzer water	Electrolytes

Drinks you should avoid: a strict no to the following drinks.

Sodas	Juices	Sweetened tea
Sports drinks	Alcohol	Sweetened coffee

Now as you are aware of what to purchase and what to avoid, it is high time that you grab your shopping back and hit the nearby grocery store. Once you have stuffed your fridge with all the low-carb foods, you will start the meal prep. Let us discuss that in the coming chapter.

Chapter 3: Meal Prep for Low-carb Diet

Taking up the low-carb diet challenge is a smart choice and even more so with so many amazing food choices.

However, don't you want to leave no stone unturned in emerging out successfully from your low-carb diet plan? If yes, here is a chapter you should consider giving a thorough read.

Knowing the plan is one thing. Executing it is an excellent way is the other. This is where meal prep comes into play.

What is Meal Prep?

Well, don't you want to sustain through the weeks of low-carb meal cooking without getting frustrated? If yes, then consider prepping your meals in advance.

Meal prepping implies preparing some of your meals or parts of a meal in advance. Suppose, you plan to cook a meal that requires a drizzle of certain condiment. If you have kept it ready beforehand, it is an act of meal prep.

In the same way, you plan to cook beef chops and you marinate the beef in advance, it is an act of meal prep.

It is a wonderful idea because it saves a lot of time and ensures you a healthy meal. As you have ample healthy low-carbs meals cooked, sticking to the plan without any deviations becomes easy.

Benefits of Meal Prep on Low-carb Diet

If you want to extract all the benefits of a low-carb meal, make sure you practice meal prepping. By doing so, not only will you have plenty of healthy foods cooked and stuffed in your fridge, you will concentrate on work, workout in the gym, and enjoy with friends.

Here are a few marvelous benefits of low-carb meal prepping.

Meal prepping is a great way to save money. You purchase food items in bulk and utilize the space of your freezer. You select a day of the week for meal prepping, execute the plan, and cook food in big volumes.

You can perform multiple tasks simultaneously. If you are a working individual, nothing like meal prepping for you. After cleaning the kitchen mess, who wants to start all about again?Nobody, I guess.

You won't feel lost and confused at the grocery store. As per the list provided in the last chapter, you can plan your weekly meals and bring the much-required variation.

You can keep a check on the portion of the macros. Meal prepping is a great way to keep a track of what is going into your stomach. It lets you know how many grams of protein, fats, and carbs a recipe contains.

A good meal prepping is the one in which a single meal is taken care of. Select a breakfast day and cook a few breakfasts and throw into the deep freeze. Reserve a day for lunch, one for condiments, one for chopping veggies, freezing herbs and berries, and the like.

Must-have Meal Prep Utensils

There are a few kitchen gears that are absolutely necessary when you consider meal prepping. Here is a list of the ultimate meal prepping kitchen tools.

Good-quality kitchen knives:

Have a set of good quality knives that allow you to chop, dice, slice, and cut veggies, meat loves, and other things.

Measuring cups and spoons:

When you cook meals that require keeping a track of macros like your low-carb high-fat meals, you need to measure the ingredients and serving size. Thus, a set of measuring cups and spoons is indispensable in your kitchen.

Food scales:

Though measuring cups and spoons can suffice, there are a few ingredients that require more accurate measures. For that, digital food scales are useful.

Kitchen utilities:

All the utilities shown in the image above like tongs, wooden spoons, whisk, etc. are very helpful in meal prep. Make sure you keep these in your kitchen pantry.

Cutting boards:

Most of the meal prepping involve a lot of chopping, dicing, slicing, and cutting. A good quality chopping board is important in your kitchen.

Mixing bowls:

Mixing the ingredients is a prerequisite for many recipes. So, keep the mixing bowls of various sizes handy.

Colander:

Rinsing veggies or fruits is necessary to eat clean and fresh foods. Buy a pair of plastic or steel colander.

Grater:

It is a great meal prepping gadget that allows you to blend the flavors of multiple ingredients together.

Baking dishes:

Your kitchen should have a set of cooking dishes. A cake pan, loaf pan, and muffin pan will help you cook multiple breakfast, dinner, desserts, and lunch recipes.

Non-stick skillet:

You cook almost everything in a skillet with a drizzle of a oil. Keep a pair of good quality skillets handy in your kitchen.

Iron cast skillet

An iron skillet is a must-have kitchen tool. It works from stove to the oven and creates some marvelous recipes.

Sauté pans:
Without a sauté pan, making sauces, cooking veggies, and creating yummy soups will be impossible.

Sheet pans:
These are extremely helpful in baking muffins, cakes etc. Buy these and place in your pantry.

Roasting pan:
From roasting chicken to beef, lamb, or fish, the roasting rack is absolutely necessary for your kitchen.

Spiralizer:
The new trend in the market is to make low-carb veg noodles known as zoodles. To make these, a spiralizer is required.

Food- processor:
Many recipes like smoothies, shakes, and condiments require a high-quality pulse or blend. Keep a food processor in your kitchen always ready.

Crockpot:
The crockpot is a one-man army. It is known for its"set and forget" style cooking that helps you create a lot of interesting recipes with literally no effort.

Meal prep containers:
To store and preserve your prepared meals, you need the right type of containers. After all, you need to keep your food preserved for the whole week.

Once, your pantry is ready, it is time for some action. Let us exercise some meal prepping ideas in the next chapter.

Chapter 4: Some Amazing Meal Prep Ideas

Have you heard the old saying, "those who fail to prepare, prepare to fail"? Well, that holds true for low-carb diet program too. Without meal prepping, things may become difficult for you to handle and you may end up quitting the program.

In today's busy life, it is really hard to spend a lot of time in kitchen, cooking variety of meals that the low-carb diet demands. What is the result? Slowly and surely the easily available junk creeps into your menu. Here meal prepping comes to your rescue.

Choosing to prepare a meal in advance especially the ones where you are in a lot of hurry is a great idea. Suppose your morning is really a hush-hush affair and you grab a takeaway breakfast, in that case prepping your breakfast is good to start with. You can subsequently prep your lunch, dinner, and even snacks.

This way, you eat a lot of healthy food throughout the week and that too tirelessly. Here are a few easy and promising meal prep steps that will show positive effects on your health and make you more organized in the kitchen.

Step 1- Meal prepping utensils

As already discussed in the last chapter, it is important for you to buy a few high quality containers wherein you can hygienically store your cooked food for the coming meals. Select a container that is microwave safe because you have to reheat the food before eating. I always recommend buying many containers of the same size that yield identical servings. This makes stacking easy too.

Step 2- Plan your recipes in advance

This is the most critical of all the steps as your entire meal prepping depends on this. When you are aware in advance of what you are going to cook in the coming week, you do not senselessly roam in the supermarket throwing everything that you find into your cart and then crossing your fingers and hoping for the best. Rather, you know your menu, ingredients, and measurements well in advance.

As I beginner, you should not overexert yourself. It may be difficult to cook for a whole week, so, cook for a few days instead. That will make it manageable and less tiresome. Once you get used to meal prepping, you can cook several meals in less time.

Go through some quick recipes and know more about the meal prep combos. Write down the recipes for the coming 3 days and make a list of the required ingredients. Select the recipes that can last long without getting spoiled. Keep taste as your primary prerequisite. Cook the foods that are healthy and taste amazing. Add flavors with homemade low-carb condiments and frozen herbs. Expand the circle of variety. Eating a same kind of food everyday will soon look boring. Try new spices and shuffle your proteins regularly.

Step 3- Allot a meal prep time slot

For beginners, I recommend meal prepping for just a few days, but how much time you dedicate to this task is absolutely up to you.

You can keep a whole day for this task or a few hours daily. You can also utilize a few hours from your Sunday to cook for the coming few days. The time you dedicate in the kitchen largely depends on what you are cooking.

Meal prepping for salads and veggie sticks is less time consuming as all you need to do is chopping the veggies and dumping them in your fridge. On the other hand, complex dishes like stews and soups may take longer hours.

Step 4- Go for the action

Meal prepping doesn't necessarily mean cooking the whole meal. Doing parts of a meal is also counted as meal prepping. Marinating chicken, meat, and fish, making chicken, bone, and vegetable broth, chopping veggies, parboiling and freezing veggies, freezing berries and herbs, preparing homemade condiments, dressings, and drizzles are all parts of meal prepping.

Even if you are not cooking in advance but the veggies are chopped, broth is ready; condiments are prepared, and chicken in marinated, consider 70% of your job done. The only thing you need at the time of cooking is combining everything and that is it. You are done!

Great meal prep ideas

In this section, I have mentioned some meal prepping ideas that will help you understand how to go about the process.

Breakfast meal prep

Poaching eggs

Pre-cooking eggs

Soaking oats

Keeping pancake dough ready

Keeping dressings and condiments prepared

Snack meal prepping

Portioningberries and hummus

Keeping nuts and seeds ready in a separate container

Portioning yogurt, whipping cream, and other ingredients

Lunch meal prepping

Assembling ingredients

Chopping veggies

Marinating chicken and mutton

Making bone and chicken broth

Dinner meal prepping

Cooking chicken ahead

Portioning veggies and salads

I am ending this chapter on the note that you are well aware of what meal prepping is and how to practice it. Make meal prepping your routine till it becomes your lifestyle. Go ahead and all the best.

In the next chapter, I will provide you with some effective tips and a few points of caution for a successful meal prep. Keep reading.

Chapter 5: Tips and Cautions of Low-carb Meal Prep

Tips of a low-carb diet

Ditching your old carb buddy and making a new fat-friend is a large scale metabolic change. Your entire system goes through a complex situation and our body takes time to accept the transition. However, there are a few tips you can keep in mind to make the transition as smooth as possible.

Quickly go through the tips given below.

<u>Divide your food into three meals and two snacks:</u> make sure you don't starve yourself for hours together. Have three meals and two snacks a day. Not eating something for hours turns you voraciously hungry and you may end up compromising on your low-carb diet.

<u>Consume carbs between 20-50grams per day:</u> neither override the daily allowance nor eat below that. Though once a while consuming 55-60grams is acceptable, but not as a routine. Similarly, going below 20grams won't help you any better. Select the right carbs from the list provided in chapter 2.

<u>Consume adequate proteins:</u> proteins keep your lean muscles supple. Consume them adequately. A serving of 4-6ounces per day is a must. At the same time, don't overeat the proteins. Balance is a must. Always remember that.

<u>Eat fats in abundance:</u> fats are the primary source of energy to your body when to switch over to the low-carb diet. So, taking healthy fats in bulk is necessary. The catch is the choose the right kind of fats. The little carb you are taking should always be accompanied with some fat.

<u>You water target should be 8 glasses of 8-ounce per day:</u> nothing like a glass of water. Set a target of 8 glasses in a day. If it is too much for you, replace a few with tea, coffee, bone, chicken, or vegetable stock.

<u>Remain hydrates all the time by keeping your electrolytes balanced:</u> electrolyte imbalance can lead to a drop in energy and dehydration. To avoid this scenario, consume foods rich in potassium, magnesium, zinc, and selenium. Add an extra dash of salt to your salad. This will help a lot.

<u>Expose the hidden carbs: food labels lie.</u> Don't be fooled by the "no-carb or low-carb" label. Check the nutritional information for a reliable source and enquire before eating at the restaurants.

<u>Use a quality sugar substitute:</u> use Stevia or monk fruit powder in moderation as a sugar substitute. Don't take in every meal and restrict the intake.

Consume only the acceptable foods: the list provided in chapter 2 should be your bible for the low-carb meals. Eat only what you are allowed to and avoid what you shouldn't. Compromising on the foods will render your low-carb practice worthless.

Cautions of a low-carb diet

As I already mentioned, going low-carb is a large-scale metabolic change, it is sensible that you take a few cautions in advance.

Take care of the following things that I have mentioned below

Be cautious about your low-carb approach. Don't switch to a low-carb meal suddenly. Start with breakfast. Switch your regular toast and oatmeal with eggs and yogurt. Adjust with breakfast first and then move to the next meal.

As a precaution, switch to low-carb snacks first. See how your body adapts to low-carb snacks. Buy plenty of them from the store and munch them instead of regular high-carb snacks. This will serve two purposes. First, you will see the reaction of your body to a low-carb meal and secondly, low-carb snacks can motivate you to switch other meals too.

Water is a known rescue ranger. The change in diet can have a substantial effect on your digestive system. Problems are bound to happen and drinking plenty of water can help you deal with them.

As a precaution against constipation, incorporate bulk of fiber in your food. A high-fat and low-carb diet can cause constipation. A portion of greens in your diet is a great idea to avoid it.

As a caution against eating too many or too less carbs, consider using a nutrition calculator. It helps you to keep a track of your carb intake and you can decrease the carb intake gradually week by week till you adapt to the new low-carb diet pattern.

To avoid going energy deficit, monitor your fat intake. Know that almost 70-85% of your calories should come from the fats alone. An extra drizzle of olive oil in your salad or the fat in nuts and avocado shouldn't bother you much. Your body needs it when you go carb-slow. Consuming less fats can eventually make you hunger and you will fall prey to the irresistible high-carb foods.

Take due precautions against the hidden carbs. You sit and enjoy of steak with a lot of veggies happily not considering the sauce that you just drizzled on the steak. You might not realize, but that sauce can contain whopping amounts of carb. Before consuming any food, get its nutritional facts checked.

Prevention is better than cure. What will you fall for if there is not high-carb food stuffed in your fridge? Nothing. It is better not to buy the high-carb foods in the first place. So, when you feel notorious, you won't have a choice except to nibble on a piece of 100% dark chocolate or some berries with cream.

As a caution against low blood sugar due to less carb intake, make sure you keep a watch of your blood sugar levels. Carry some glucose tablets with you to deal with a panicky situation.

Make the changes gradually. Lower sugar step by step. 2 cubes of sugar in your coffee should become 1 and then nil. 3 tsp of ketchup should become 2, then 1 and then nil. This makes the change enduring.

In the next chapter, I will discuss some common mistakes you are expected to make while following a low-carb diet and how to avoid those.

Chapter 6: Common Mistakes You Must Avoid

As silly as it sounds, there are some unexpectedly common mistakes people make when they switch to a low-carb diet. These small mistakes make a large impact. They have the ability to slow down the entire process and even render it ineffective. In the first chapter, I have already discussed a few prominent mistakes that low-carb dieters make. In this chapter, I want to move a step further and count the least noticed mistakes that seem little but can cause serious glitches to a low-carb dieter like you.

Let us counter these mistakes one and one and make sure you don't fall for these during your low-carb journey.

Eating too little or no carbs: let me keep it simple. Little carb means little carb, it doesn't mean no carb. When you go on a low-carb diet, ensure that you consume all the macros including carbs. Yes, I know carbs are to be consumed in small portions, but it doesn't mean they are not to be consumed at all. If you think that going carb-free will yield you quick and better results, rethink.

Overconsuming fats and proteins: this is yet another silly but common mistake. It is a fact that you must keep the carbs low and derive most of your nutrition from fats, but it never means that you should overeat the two allowed macros.

Eating meat, dairy, and cheese ravenously will double your health risks and reverse lead to weight gain. If you think that low-carb is a certificate to eat proteins and fats limitlessly, you are wrong.

Skipping veggies and fruits: in an advent to lower the carb intake, it is seen that most of the dieters stop consuming veggies and fruit. This is absolutely wrong. Veggies are not good but great for your low-carb diet.

Citrus fruits and berries complete your low-carb diet. Fruits are exceptionally rich in vitamins and minerals that maintain the health of your body and reduce your vulnerability against several chronic illnesses. Thus, don't forget to stuff your plate with a portion of veggies and fruits.

Being fat-phobic: the poor guy known as fat has always suffered a bad reputation of being mischievous. Most of us blame fat for causing weight gain and many other chronic diseases. This, however, is a partial fact. The truth is that fats some fats are bad while others are good. Thus, not consuming the right fats is as disastrous for your body as over-consuming them.

Healthy fats like omega-3fatty acids have a noteworthy effect on the development of your brain and cardiovascular functioning. So, don't be afraid of fats. Select the right kind of fat in a right proportion. Believe me, you will see the benefits coming in no time.

Overlooking fiber: fruits and veggies promise a great amount of fiber in your diet. When you go carb-slow, you become vulnerable to develop gastrointestinal disorders for some time till you adapt to the high-fat regime. Fiber is the best precaution you can take in such a situation. Make sure you get a genuine portion of low-carb high-fiber in your diet. Flax seeds and chia seeds are quite rich in fiber.

Not planning ahead: falling for the old habits is quite anticipated especially in the initial days of the low-carb diet. So, the right thing would be to relax and reconsider your habits. You can no longer carelessly go and make yourself a mug of coffee with 3 sugar cubes popped in, nor can you munch your favorite bar of chocolate.

Planning is a precaution till your new habits naturally flow. You feel hungry and you have many low-carb foods stuffed in your fridge. You will at once grab one. This is something known as planning.

Planning your weekly meals before hitting the grocery store, practicing meal prepping, and keeping low-carb snacks handy are a few examples to name.

Getting into a routine: there are very few who can eat a particular food every day and not get bored. I am sure you are not one of those. Most of us are in desperate need of variety. To avoid boredom from the low-carb diet, I strongly suggest trying as many varieties as you can. And why not? Every cuisine has a big range of low-carb recipes. Go for a few.

Believing the low-carb label: don't go over the cloud nine if someone tells you about the low-carb or no-carb sweets, ice cream, chocolates, and what not. These contain maltitol which is as bad as sugar. Also, be cautious about the products that talk too much about net-carbs and impact-carbs. Scrutinize the ingredients thoroughly before buying.

Taking is easy: so, you are going carb-slow, losing weight, looking fresh, concentrating, and not feeling hungry and everything is just perfect. Then, you think how does it matter if I have a piece of toast or a little sugar in my tea. Guess what, you are wrong.

You don't realize, but your body has set its personal carb limit and it is going fine on it. As you take it easy, you at once gain weight, get cravings and feel hungrier. To avoid the vicious cycle of carb creep-in, don't take it way too easy.

Bunking exercise: you may lose weight initially without exercising but exercising regularly has plenty of benefits like it lowers insulin resistance, helps to shed weight easily, and keeps you fit.

In the next chapter, I will address a few FAQs. Keep reading dear friends.

Chapter 7: Frequently Asked Questions

I have addressed a few questions in the first chapter, in this chapter I have addressed a few more quires that you probably encounter while going low-carb.

Q: When it comes to weight loss, I have always heard of the calories in and calories out principle. It that right?

A: No. It sadly isn't. Weight loss is determined by the type of food you consume because food has a lot to do with hormones, appetite control, and fat metabolism. When you go carb-slow, you choose fat as the primary fuel of your body. On the other hand, if you consume less calories, you feel hungry and then fall for high-carb foods. Thus, losing weight by switching over to a high-fat diet is a long-term approach as compared to cutting calories which is short-term.

Q: Is eliminating a major macro sensible?

A: please understand the difference between a low-carb diet and a carb-free diet. Eating low-carbs means rationally avoiding high ends carbs like wheat, grains, and sugar. You still get your share of carbs in the form of low-carb fruits, berries, non-starchy veggies, and other natural foods. Thus, the negative impact of the carbs on your body is avoided and you have a much stable insulin level, better appetite control, and a healthy hormonal profile.

Q: Is avoiding grains important?

A:The grains that you have now are not the same that your grandfather used to have. Grains are no less destructive than refined sugar. These are now consumed in the form of processed foods, bread, cakes, pasta, cookies, and rice which are very high-end carbs. It implies that if you get rid of grains, you drastically reduce your carb intake which intake balances your insulin levels and controls the onset of hunger. Before taking up the low-carb diet, talk to your doctor. You may need to reduce your medication if you plan to go for a low-carb diet.

Q: Eating more fats causes weight loss. I have always heard the opposite. Are you sure that is true?

A: Yes, I know the decade-old myth. Eat less fat to shed weight. This principle is unfortunately backed up by poor scientific logic. The fact remains that if you eat healthy fats in abundance like olive oil, coconut oil, avocado, and butter, you remain full for a longer period, have a stable hormonal profile, and face fewer carb cravings.

Q: Carbs are the primary fuel sources for our body. How do you justify going low-carb?

A: that is not right. Humans are the best-known adapters. Our ancestors have survived through the phases of large level mutations and the current human civilization is a proof of that. Changing from a high-carb to high-fat diet is comparatively a very small change. Don't worry, your body will soon adapt to the fat as primary fuel and run effectively. An unlimited supply of energy from fat instead of glucose is a positive change.

Q: Instead of eliminating carbs, can I eat everything in moderation?
A: The thing is that nobody can "eat in moderation" for long. It is an easy excuse to get rid of a diet schedule. Instead, have a treat once a week. That is justified and understandable. Eating everything in moderation is something I won't recommend.

Q: Is consuming so much fat acceptable for my cardiovascular functioning?
A: This is a common myth. There are thousands like you who believe this myth to be true. Scientific research proves the opposite, however. Not fat but high-carb intake increases chances of cardiovascular problems. The catch is to select the healthy fats instead of the unhealthy ones. Increase the intake of monosaturated fats like olive oil, butter, and the like. They are highly beneficial and cause literally no harm.

Q: Guide me on my cholesterol level?
A: Cholesterol is extremely important as it is the building block for many hormones. It is an indispensable part of your body cells. The fact, however, is that not cholesterol but the inflammation of the arteries is the major cause of heart diseases and nothing causes inflammation more than a diet rich in carbs and sugar.

Q: How should I plan my low-carb diet?
A: Firstly, eliminate the junk. Next comes the snacks followed by one meal at a time like breakfast, then lunch, and the like. At the same time incorporate nuts, seeds, and plenty of low-carb fruits in your diet. Increase healthy fat intake. If you plan and stick to it, benefits will start flowing quickly and easily. Trust me on that.

Now, your concept about the low-carb diet and how it functions is clear. It is time for some real action now. In the coming chapters, I will put forth a few mouth-watering low-carb recipes that you can try. So, dear readers, adjust your chef's hat. It is time to cook.

Chapter 8-Low-carb breakfast ideas

Egg with cheese soldiers

This is an ultimate low-carb high-fat breakfast to give a great start to your day.

Calories: 271 kcal
Proteins: 17.6 grams
Total carbs: 1.1grams
Fat: 21.5grams
Servings: 1
Ingredients:

● 1 egg
● 50g full- fat cheese
● Salt

Preparation:

1. Put eggs in a vessel and allow it to boil.
2. Grate the eggs and set aside.
3. Melt the cheese in a pan and cook for a couple of minutes.
4. Add a dash of salt and transfer the grated eggs into it.
5. Sauté for 2 minutes and serve.

1-minute keto muffin

It is the tastiest and healthiest single serving muffin you can make in no time.

Calories: 113 kcal
Proteins: 7 grams
Total carbs: 5grams
Fat: 11grams
Servings: 1
Ingredients:

● 1 egg
● 2 tsp coconut flour and butter
● Pinch of baking soda and salt

Preparation:

1. Melt some butter in a pan.
2. Mix all the ingredients in a bowl and combine into a fine dough.
3. Transfer the dough to a greased pan and spread it evenly. Bake at 400F for 12 minutes. Slice and serve.

Breakfast asparagus

Quick to cook and yummy to taste. Give this recipe a try.

Calories: 216kcal
Proteins: 14 grams
Total carbs: 3.5grams
Fat: 28grams
Servings: 1
Ingredients:
- 2 diced bacon slices
- 6 trimmed asparagus sprigs
- 2 eggs
- 1/2 tbsp chopped chives
- Salt and pepper

Preparation:
1. Cook bacon in a pan for 5 minutes until crisp and set aside.
2. Put the asparagus in the pan and cook till it turns tender.
3. Break 2 eggs over the cooked asparagus and season it with salt, pepper, and chives.
4. Sauté till eggs are done and top it with diced bacon. Serve.

Cream cheese pancakes

If there is a best low-carb pancake recipe, it is this.

Calories: 344kcal
Proteins: 17 grams
Total carbs: 5grams
Fat: 29grams
Servings: 4
Ingredients:
- 2 oz cream cheese
- 2 eggs
- 1 tsp Stevia
- 1/2tsp cinnamon

Preparation:
1. Blends all the ingredients until smooth.
2. Pour a little batter into a greased hot pan.
3. Cook for 4 minutes on both sides till golden. Repeat the same for the remaining batter.
4. Top with berries and serve with a drizzle of sugar-free syrup.

Avocado and salmon low -carb breakfast

A simple yet delicious recipe that is a perfect breakfast choice.

Calories: 525kcal

Proteins: 19grams

Total carbs: 4grams

Fat: 48grams

Servings: 1

Ingredients:

- 1 ripe avocado
- 60 grams smoked salmon
- 30 grams fresh goat cheese
- 2 tablespoon olive oil
- 1 tsp lemon juice
- Salt

Preparation:

1. Cut the avocado in cubes and salmon in small pieces and combine.
2. Add cheese and the rest of the ingredients.
3. Blend the mixture in the food processor until coarsely chopped and serve.

Peanut butter power granola

Try this recipe and it will take a permanent place in your low-carb breakfast menu.

Calories: 338kcal

Proteins:9.3grams

Total carbs: 9grams

Fat: 30grams

Servings: 12

Ingredients:

● 1-1/2 cup almonds and pecans
● 1 cup almond flour
● 1/4 cup sunflower seeds
● 1/3 cup Stevia
● 1/3 cup protein powder and peanut butter
● 1/4 cup butter and water

Preparation:

1. Preheat oven to 300F and line it with baking sheet.
2. Pulse almonds and pecans in a mixer into coarse crumbs.
3. Transfer it to a bowl and add shredded coconut, sunflower seeds, Stevia and vanilla powder.
4. Melt the butter in a microwave bowl.
5. Pour melted butter mixture and water over nut mixture and combine.
6. Evenly spread the mixture on baking sheet and bake for 30 minutes.
7. Cool and serve.

Lemon poppy seed breakfast cookies

These protein boost cookies make a great breakfast especially if you are running late for work.

Calories: 189kcal

Proteins:5.8grams

Total carbs: 7.5grams

Fat: 15.03grams

Servings: 8

Ingredients:

- 1 cup almond flour
- 1/4 cup coconut flour
- 3 tbsp poppy seeds
- 1 tsp baking powder
- Salt
- 6 ounces softened cheese cream
- 1/2 cup confectioners sweetener
- I egg
- 2 tsp lemon juice
- 1/4tsp liquid stevia extracts

Preparation:

1. Preheat oven to 325F and line it with baking sheet.
2. Mix almond flour, coconut flour, poppy seeds, baking powder, and salt together.
3. Beat cheese cream, sweetener, egg, lemon juice and Stevia extract and mix it with above mixture until well combined.
4. Make 8 to 10 even balls from the batter.
5. Bake for 20 minutes till brown. Let it cool. Enjoy.

Mini –smoked salmon frittatas

These small power-packed frittatas are a good light breakfast option or a good on-the-go munch.

Calories: 179kcal
Proteins:17grams
Total carbs: 3grams
Fat: 11grams
Servings: 1

Ingredients:

- 1tbsp olive oil
- 1/4 cup chopped onion
- Salt and pepper
- 4 ounces smoked salmon cut into pieces
- 6 eggs
- 8 egg whites
- 3 tbsp milk
- 3 ounces cubed less fat cream cheese
- 2tbsp thinly sliced scallions

Preparation:

1. Preheat oven to 325F.
2. Sauté onion for 2-3 minutes in some oil.
3. Add salt, pepper, and salmon. Set aside.
4. Combine rest of the ingredients in a bowl.
5. Stir it in the cream cheese.
6. Light coat 6 ramekins with cooking spray.
7. Add some salmon mixture and topped with egg mixture to each ramekin.
8. Bake for 25 minutes till done and garnish.

Peppermint protein shake

The energy-packed shake tastes delicious and gives a perfect start to the day.

Calories: 200kcal

Proteins:39grams

Total carbs: 7grams

Fat: 2grams

Servings: 1

Ingredients:

- 1/2 cup fat-free cottage cheese
- 2 tbsp cocoa powder
- 1/4 cup vanilla protein powder
- 2-4 drops peppermint extract
- 1 tsp stevia
- Water and ice cubes as desired

Preparation:

1. Put all the ingredients in a mixer and blend into a shake.
2. Garnish it with mint leaves and enjoy.

Cinnamon Roll Scones

If you are late for work, this quick breakfast recipe is your savior and it tastes yummy.

Calories: 252kcal
Proteins:6.7grams
Total carbs: 7.1grams
Fat: 23grams
Servings: 8 scones

Ingredients:

Scones:
- 2 cups almond flour
- 3 tbsp sweetener
- 2 tsp baking powder
- Salt
- 1/4 cup ground cinnamon
- 1 lightly beaten egg
- 1/4 cup coconut oil or butter
- 1/2 cup vanilla extract

Filling/Topping:
- 3 tbsp sweetener
- 2 tsp cinnamon

Icing:
- 1 Oz softened cream cheese
- 1 tbsp cream
- 1/2 tbsp softened butter
- 1 tbsp sweetener
- 1/4 tsp vanilla extract

Preparation:

Scones
1. Preheat oven to 325F and line it with a baking sheet.
2. In a bowl put almond flour, sweetener, baking powder, salt, cinnamon and mix it.
3. Add in egg, coconut oil, cream and vanilla extract and mix.
4. Whisk together filling ingredients and add half of filling into dough and mix it.
5. Give the dough a rough shape and add the remaining topping. Slice into even shapes and separate.
6. Bake for 25 minutes till scones are firm and light brown.

Icing:
1. Beat cream cheese, butter, and cream until smooth.
2. Put powdered sweetener and vanilla extract and combine.
3. Spread the mixture over cooled scones.

Chapter 9 – Low-carb lunch and dinner ideas

Healthy and delicious low-carb lunch recipes

Dijon broccoli chicken

This flavorful and delicious lunch takes just 30minutes to cook.

Calories: 185 kcal

Proteins: 29.2 grams

Total carbs: 5.05grams

Fat: 5.27grams

Servings: 1

Ingredients:

- 1/2 cup chicken broth
- 1 tbsp soy sauce, olive oil
- 4 cups broccoli
- 1 clove garlic, minced
- 1 lb chicken breasts
- 6 tsp Dijon mustard

Preparation:

1. Mix chicken broth and soy sauce and set aside.
2. Cook broccoli and garlic in oil until crisp.
3. Cook chicken in the skillet and pour the broth mixture.
4. Bring the contents to a boil and stir in mustard.
5. Add the fried broccoli and cook till done. Serve.

Cheesy beef bake

This is a very satisfying lunch idea that tastes delicious at the same time.

Calories: 304 kcal

Proteins: 40 grams

Total carbs: 6.5grams

Fat: 12.4grams

Servings: 1

Ingredients:

- 1 lb minced beef
- 5 large eggs
- 1 cup chopped spinach
- 1/4 cup chopped red bell pepper
- 4 Oz shredded cheddar cheese
- Salt
- Pepper

Preparation:

1. Preheat oven to 350 F.
2. Cook ground beef till brown.
3. Add red bell pepper and spinach and mix.
4. Transfer the mixture into a baking dish and spread.
5. Whisk eggs, salt, and pepper in a bowl and pour over beef mixture.
6. Top with cheddar cheese.
7. Bake for 20 minutes.
8. Cut into slices before serving.

Italian-style baked mushrooms

Serve this appetizing dish along with a lot of salad to have a great low-carb lunch.

Calories: 232 kcal

Proteins: 14.3 grams

Total carbs: 9grams

Fat: 15grams

Servings: 4

Ingredients:

- 500g sliced mushrooms
- 1 can tomatoes
- 2 cups grated parmesan cheese
- 2 tbsp ghee and basil
- 1 tbsp parsley
- 1 tsp dried oregano
- Salt
- Pepper

Preparation:

1. Preheat oven to 200C.
2. Fry the mushrooms in ghee for 5 minutes and add a dash of salt and pepper.
3. Place mushrooms in a baking tray.
4. In a bowl, mix spices, salt, pepper, and tomatoes and pour on the mushrooms.
5. Top with cheese and bake for 25 minutes. Serve.

Roasted cauliflower with mozzarella cheese

The cheese filled cauliflower dish makes a great and hunger-satisfying lunch.

Calories: 129 kcal
Proteins: 7.2 grams
Total carbs: 6grams
Fat: 10.8grams
Servings: 8

Ingredients:
- 1 clean large head cauliflower, washed and sliced
- 2 tbsp oil or melted coconut
- 2 tbsp fresh thyme
- Dash of salt and pepper
- 1 head roasted garlic

Preparation:
1. Preheat oven to 425F.Put the cauliflower evenly on a baking sheet.
2. Sprinkle oil evenly over the cauliflower and add salt, pepper, and garlic and toss to combine.
3. Roast till the cauliflower is caramelized for about 30 minutes.
4. Garnish it with cheese and thyme leaves.

Garlic parmesan fried eggplant

I have never come across a dish that makes you fall for eggplant more than this.

Calories: 271 kcal
Proteins: 12 grams
Servings: 6

Total carbs: 9grams
Fat: 22grams

Ingredients:
- 1 sliced eggplant
- Salt
- Pepper
- 1 egg
- 1 cup almond flour and parmesan cheese
- 2 tsp garlic powder
- 1/2 cup oil

Preparation:
1. Sprinkle the sliced eggplant with salt and set aside.
2. Blot eggplant dry.
3. In one bowl whisk egg and in other bowl combine almond flour, garlic powder, salt, and pepper.
4. Dip each slice of eggplant in egg and then in almond flour mixture.
5. Fry the eggplant slices in some oil until crispy and serve.

Quick and easy low-carb dinner recipes

Egg stuffed avocado

Avocados stuffed with diced eggs and a lot of cheese is definitely a mouth-watering lunch.

Calories: 400 kcal
Proteins: 16.5 grams
Total carbs: 9.5grams
Fat: 40grams
Servings: 2
Ingredients:
- 2pitted avocados
- 4 boiled eggs
- 1/4 cup mayonnaise
- 2 tbsp cream cheese
- 1 tsp Dijon mustard
- 2 sliced spring onions
- Salt
- Pepper

Preparation:
1. Dice the boiled eggs.
2. Combine all the ingredients in a bowl and add the diced eggs to it.
3. Scoop out the flesh of the avocado and cut into small pieces.
4. In a bowl, thoroughly mix the chopped avocado with eggs.
5. Fill each half avocado with the mixture. Serve.

Mushroom risotto

Portobello mushrooms cooked with a plenty of low-carb ingredients is a recipe worth trying.

Calories: 264 kcal
Proteins: 11.9 grams
Total carbs: 10.5grams
Fat: 17.1grams
Servings: 4
Ingredients:

- 4-1/2 cups cauliflower, riced
- 3 tbsp oil or butter
- 1 lb Portobello and white mushrooms, thinly sliced
- 2 diced shallots
- 1/4 cup veggie broth
- Salt
- Pepper
- 3 tbsp chopped chives
- 4 tbsp butter
- 1/3 cup grated parmesan cheese

Preparation:

1. Cook mushrooms, shallots, and cauliflower rice for 5 minutes in some oil.
2. Add broth and boil the contents reduce.
3. Remove from heat and stir mushrooms with butter, chives, and parmesan.
4. Season with salt and pepper.

Buffalo potato wedges with blue cheese drizzle

This recipe is a very filling, delicious, and healthy. Go for it.

Calories: 235 kcal

Proteins: 2.5grams

Total carbs: 10grams

Fat: 15grams

Servings: 1

Ingredients:

- 2 clean and peeled rutabagas
- 4 tbsp butter
- 1/2 tsp onion powder
- Salt
- Pepper
- 1/2 cup buffalo wing sauce
- 1/4 cup cheese
- 2 green onions chopped

Preparation:

1. Preheat oven to 400F.
2. Slice rutabagas into wedges.
3. Melt butter and spices and coat rutabagas wedges with it.
4. Put wedges on a baking sheet and bake for 30 minutes.
5. Remove and toss with buffalo wing sauce and bake for other 15 minutes.
6. Top with cheese and green onions. Serve.

Keto garlic gnocchi

Gnocchi with plenty of cheese and garlic is one of its kind. This dish is definitely going to make it to your low-carb menu.

Calories: 250 kcal
Proteins: 12grams
Total carbs: 9.5grams
Fat: 20grams
Servings: 2

Ingredients:

- 2 cups mozzarella shredded
- 3 egg yolks
- 1 tsp granulated garlic
- butter and olive oil

Preparation:

1. Combine molten cheese and garlic in a bowl.
2. Add yolks and make the dough. Portion dough into 4 balls.
3. Refrigerate for 1o minutes.
4. Roll each ball into a log.
5. Slice each log into 1-inch gnocchi.
6. Boil water with salt and place the gnocchi into it.
7. Sauté the boiled gnocchi in some butter and oil till they turn golden brown.
Serve.

Grain-free Mac and cheese

This low-carb dish is nothing short of a delight. Give it a try.

Calories: 400 kcal

Proteins: 25grams

Total carbs: 12grams

Fat: 40grams

Servings: 4

Ingredients:

- 1/2 crème Fraiche and heavy crème
- 2 tbsp yellow mustard
- Salt
- Pepper
- 1 lb jicama cut into pieces.
- 1/2 cup minced onion
- 3 cups shredded cheddar cheese

Preparation:

1. Put crème Fraiche, heavy cream, salt, pepper, yellow mustard in a bowl and mix.
2. Add in the onion and jicama and coat well.
3. Add shredded cheese and mix.
4. Put the mixture in a greased baking pan and bake at 350F for 50 minutes and serve.

Chapter 10: Low-carb Meat Recipes

Thit Bo Xao Dua

This is a yummy beef preparation cooked in beans and condiments.

Net carbs: 6.3grams

Proteins: 23.1grams

Fats: 28.6grams

Calories: 376kcal

Serving size: 4

Ingredients:

- 1 bowl beef chunks
- 1 minced garlic clove
- Pepper
- 1 tsp cornstarch
- 3 tbsp oil
- 1/2 thinly sliced onion
- 2 cups trimmed green beans
- 1/4 cup chicken stock
- 1 tsp soy sauce

Preparation:

1. Mix garlic paste, pepper, cornstarch, and oil in a bowl and add the beef chunks to it.
2. Heat oil and cook the marinated beef till it turns brown.
3. Cook onions in some oil till soft. Transfer beans and broth to it.
4. Boil till beans turn tender and add the soy sauce and beef. Serve.

Beef Stroganoff

Beef cooked in butter, cream, and sauce is a lifetime delicacy.

Net carbs: 5.7grams
Proteins: 16.6grams
Fats: 23grams
Calories: 304kcal
Serving size: 6

Ingredients:

- 2 pounds beef chuck strips
- Salt
- Pepper
- 4 ounce molten butter
- 4 sliced green onions
- 1 can beef broth
- 1 tsp mustard sauce
- 1/3 cup sour cream and vinegar

Preparation:

1. Cook the beef strips in butter till they turn brown and set aside.
2. Sauté onions till soft and take out on the beef strips.
3. Pour the broth and mustard into the pan and boil.
4. Add the beef strips and cook for an hour.
5. Stir in the vinegar, salt, pepper, and sour cream. Serve.

The best meatloaf

Baked minced mutton with a plenty of low-carb ingredients can be a perfect lunch or dinner.

Net carbs: 10.1grams
Proteins: 20.9grams
Fats: 17.9grams
Calories: 288kcal
Serving size: 6

Ingredients:

- 1/2 cup milk
- 1 cup bread crumbs
- 1-1/2 cup minced mutton
- Salt
- Pepper
- 1whisked egg
- 3 tbsp low-carb steak sauce
- 1 chopped onion
- 1/2 cup diced bell peppers

Preparation:

1. Preheat oven to 350F.
2. Dip the bread crumbs in milk till they become mushy.
3. Assemble the mutton, salt, pepper, egg, steak sauce, onion, and bell pepper in a bowl and pour the breadcrumb mixture over it.
4. Combine well and pour on a loaf pan.
5. Bake for an hour. Slice and serve.

Super delicious meatballs

Nothing tastes better than meatballs with herbs and cheese. Try it for your lunch or dinner.

Net carbs: 6.6grams

Proteins: 26.6grams

Fats: 53.2grams

Calories: 613kcal

Serving size: 8

Ingredients:

- 1 pound minced lamb meat
- 1/2 pound ground veal and pork
- 2 minced garlic cloves
- 2 eggs
- 1 cup shredded cheese
- 1-1/2 cup parsley
- Salt
- Pepper
- 1 cup warm water
- 1 cup olive oil

Preparation:

1. Mix meat, pork, and veal in a bowl. Add garlic, cheese, parsley, salt, and pepper to it and combine well.
2. Add the little warm water to the mixture and roll it into meatballs.
3. Fry the balls in oil till brown and serve.

Rolled flank steak

Marinated beef strips cooked with lots of veggies tastes yummy.

Net carbs: 3grams
Proteins: 31.4grams
Fats: 36.9grams
Calories: 472kcal
Serving size: 6

Ingredients:

- 2 pounds beef flank steak
- 1/4 cup soy sauce
- 1/2 cup olive oil
- 2 tsp steak seasoning
- 8 ounces sliced cheese
- 4 slices cut bacon
- 1/2 cup spinach and mushrooms
- 1/2 diced bell pepper

Preparation:

1. Cut the flank steaks into strips.
2. Combine soy sauce, oil, and steak seasoning in a Ziploc bag and marinate the beef overnight.
3. Preheat the oven to 350F.
4. Layer the beef strips with cheese, bacon, spinach, bell pepper, and mushrooms and roll the strips into a wheel.
5. Bake the beef wheels for 15 minutes at 145F. Serve.

Foolproof rib roast

A simple yet marvelous recipe of roasted ribs with minimal spices is a great side dish.

Net carbs: 0.6grams   **Fats: 46.2grams**
Proteins: 37grams   **Calories: 576kcal**
Serving size: 6

Ingredients:

- 1 pound lamb or beef ribs
- Salt
- Pepper
- 1 tsp garlic powder

Preparation:

1. Preheat the oven to 375F.
2. Mix salt, pepper, and garlic powder in a small bowl.
3. Adjust the ribs on a grill with the fatty side up.
4. Thoroughly season it with the spice mix.
5. Roast for an hour and let it rest in the oven for 3 hours.
6. Before serving, roast it again for 30 minutes.

London broil

Marinated and grilled steak is an amazing lunch or dinner option.

Net carbs: 1.2grams   **Fats: 20.6grams**
Proteins: 48.6grams   **Calories: 396kcal**
Serving size: 8

Ingredients:

- 1 minced garlic clove
- Salt
- 3 tbsp soy sauce
- 1 tbsp tomato puree
- 1 tbsp olive oil
- Pepper
- 1/2 tsp oregano
- 4 pounds flank steak

Preparation:

1. Combine all the ingredients in a bowl to make a fine marinade.
2. Make deep cuts into the meat and rub the marinade all over it.
3. Marinate for overnight.
4. Grease the grill with some oil and preheat it.
5. Grill the meat for 7 minutes per side till it is done. Serve.

German Rouladen

Bacon and few other ingredients rolled into a filet is a perfect low-carb recipe.

Net carbs: 7.7grams
Proteins: 19.1grams
Fats: 17.4grams
Calories: 264kcal
Serving size: 6

Ingredients:

- 1-1/2 cup lamb steak
- Ground mustard
- 1/2 pound sliced bacon
- 2 sliced onion
- 1 jar dill pickles
- 2 bsp butter
- 2-1/2 cups water
- 1 cup bone broth

Preparation:

1. Chop the flanks into filets.
2. Rub mustard on each filet on one side.
3. Adjust bacon, onions, and pickles on the fillets and make a roll of each.
4. Melt butter and sauté the rolls to brown.
5. Boil water and bone broth and add the rolls. Cook for an hour. Serve.

Jalapeno Steak

Grilled steak with a lot of jalapeno is a low-carb dish relished by all.

Net carbs: 3.1grams

Proteins: 19.1grams

Fats: 10.5grams

Calories: 186kcal

Serving size: 6

Ingredients:

- 4 sliced jalapeno
- 4 peeled garlic cloves
- Pepper
- Salt
- 1/4 cup lime juice
- 1 tbsp dried oregano
- 1-1/2 pound sirloin steak

Preparation:

1. Grind all the ingredients in a mixer into a fine blend.
2. Place the steak in a Ziploc bag and pour over the marinade.
3. Marinate overnight.
4. Preheat an oil-coated grill and adjust the marinated steak on it.
5. Grill for 5 minutes on each side till it is tender. Serve.

Mexican beef supreme

Beef cooked in plenty of veggies and herbs makes a hunger-killer dinner.

Net carbs: 8.6grams
Proteins: 30.2grams
Fats: 27.9grams
Calories: 414kcal
Serving size: 4
Ingredients:
- 1 tbsp olive oil
- 1 diced onion
- 1 pound beef stew meat
- 1 tsp minced garlic
- 2 tsp lime juice
- 1 chopped jalapeno
- 3 chopped green onions
- 1/4 cup chopped cilantro
- 1 tsp dried oregano
- 1 can green salsa

Preparation:
1. Heat oil and sauté the onions till soft.
2. Add beef and garlic and cook till beef turns brown.
3. Combine rest of the ingredients in a bowl and stir into the pot.
4. Cook for 10 minutes till meat is done. Serve.

Chapter 11: Low-carb Poultry Recipes

Italian chicken

Chicken marinated in Italian salad dressing tastes straight from heaven. Give it a try.

Net carbs: 7.7grams   **Fats: 22.4grams**

Proteins: 27.5grams   **Calories: 344kcal**

Serving size: 6

Ingredients:

- 6 chicken breast sliced into halves
- 1 bottle Italian salad dressing

Preparation:

1. Pour the salad dressing into a Ziploc bag and add the chicken breasts.
2. Shake well and marinate overnight.
3. Preheat oven to 350F.
4. Coat a baking dish with cooking spray and place the chicken pieces into it.
5. Bake for 1 hour till chicken turns juicy. Serve.

Grilled chicken with spinach and mozzarella

Chicken baked with a lot of spinach and mozzarella is a great low-carb dish.

Net carbs: 3.6grams   **Fats: 26grams**

Proteins: 31grams   **Calories: 195kcal**

Serving size: 6

Ingredients:

- 3 large chicken breasts split into half
- Salt
- Pepper
- 1 tsp olive oil
- 3 minced garlic cloves
- 10 oz fresh spinach
- 0 oz grated mozzarella
- 1/2 cup roasted red pepper strips
- Cooking spray

Preparation:

1. Preheat the oven to 400F.
2. Sprinkle some salt and pepper on the chicken pieces and grill for 3 minutes till it turns brown.
3. Sauté garlic and spinach for 5 minutes in some oil.
4. Transfer chicken to a baking pan and top with the cooked spinach.
5. Add some mozzarella and peppers and bake for 3 minutes. Serve.

Rosemary over-fried chicken

This is a unique and marvelous low-carb chicken recipe that can be a part of your lunch or dinner menu.

Net carbs: 1.8grams
Proteins: 27.4grams
Fats: 30.7grams
Calories: 248kcal
Serving size: 4

Ingredients:

- 1/4 cup full-fat buttermilk
- 2 tbsp Dijon mustard
- 4 ounce chicken cutlets
- 1/3 cup breadcrumbs
- 1/3 cup roasted cashews
- 3/4 tsp minced rosemary
- Salt
- Pepper
- Cooking spray

Preparation:

1. Preheat oven to 425F.
2. Whisk the buttermilk and mustard and add chicken to it.
3. Cook panko in a pan till it turns golden.
4. Combine it with the rest of the ingredients in a bowl and add the marinated chicken to it.
5. Bake the chicken for 25minutes.Serve.

Cheese turkey with broccoli bake

Baked broccoli served with turkey slices makes anice low-carb lunch.

Net carbs: 6grams

Proteins: 25grams

Fats: 16grams

Calories: 266kcal

Serving size: 4

Ingredients:

- 2 cups broccoli florets and chopped turkey
- 1/4 tsp all-purpose seasoning
- 1 cup grated cheddar cheese
- 5 whisked eggs

Preparation:

1. Preheat oven to 375F.
2. Bake the broccoli for 2 minutes.
3. Combine the broccoli with turkey in the same dish and add the seasoning and cheese.
4. Pour the whisked eggs into the mixture and stir well to combine.
5. Cook till eggs are done and serve.

Turkey Ratatouille

Turkey cooked with diverse veggies is a unique and delicious low-carb meal.

Net carbs: 3.9grams
Proteins: 42.7grams
Fats: 18.3grams
Calories: 391.3kcal
Serving size: 4

Ingredients:
- 24 oz turkey cutlets
- 4 tbsp olive oil
- 1 eggplant
- 1 zucchini
- 1 chopped red pepper
- 1 cup chopped mushrooms
- 1 tsp garlic paste
- 1/2 cup tomato puree
- 1 tsp dried basil
- 1/2 tsp Stevia
- Salt
- Pepper

Preparation:
1. Sauté the cutlets in some oil till they turn golden and set aside.
2. Cook the veggies, spices, Stevia, salt, and pepper in the same pan.
3. Add water and boil the contents.
4. Add the turkey cutlets back and cook for 3 minutes. Serve.

Pan fried duck breasts

This high-fat and low-carb dish made from duck breasts is a known keto recipe. Go for it.

Net carbs: 8grams
Proteins: 27grams
Fats: 50grams
Calories: 560kcal
Serving size: 1
Ingredients:
- 2 duck breasts
- 1 tbsp coconut oil
- 2 zucchinis
- 1 daikon
- 2 green bell peppers
- 1 spring onion
- Salt
- Pepper

Preparation:
1. Make deep cuts in the duck breast pieces.
2. Chop the veggies and sauté them for 5-7minutes.
3. Heat a non-stick pan and add the duck pieces to it.
4. Cook the duck breast pieces in the fat that it will shed and flip sides occasionally.
5. Adjust salt and pepper and combine the veggies with duck pieces and serve.

Duck Caesar salad

Veggies, dressings, and cheese cooked with duck breast pieces is a perfect low-carb high-fat dinner or lunch.

Net carbs: 4.1grams
Proteins: 36.7grams
Fats: 59.1grams
Calories: 707kcal
Serving size: 4

Ingredients:

- 2 duck breasts
- 8 bacon slices
- 4 heads green lettuce
- 4 servings salad dressing
- 4 oz Parmesan cheese flakes
- Salt
- Pepper
- Chia seed croutons

Preparation:

1. Bake the bacon slices and set aside.
2. Season duck breasts with salt and pepper.
3. Let the duck cook for 7 minutes in a hot pan and then roast for 15 minutes.
4. Toss the spinach, chia seeds, and cheese flakes together into a dressing.
5. Top the lettuce with the duck pieces, cheese flakes, and bacon. Serve.

Low-carb egg salad

Grated egg with mayonnaise is an easy and nice low-carb recipe.

Net carbs: 1.7grams
Proteins: 8.7grams
Fats: 12grams
Calories: 105kcal
Serving size: 4

Ingredients:

- 6 boiled eggs
- 125ml mayonnaise
- 1 tsp curry powder
- Salt
- Pepper

Preparation:

1. Remove the peel from the boiled eggs and grate them using a vegetable grater.
2. Spoon out the mayonnaise in a bowl and add the grated eggs to it.
3. Season with salt, pepper, and curry powder.
4. Combine well and serve.

Low-carb scrambled eggs

Scrambled eggs with bacon cooked in an oven serve as a nice and healthy low-carb breakfast.

Net carbs: 2.8grams
Proteins: 17.5grams
Fats: 12.3grams
Calories: 179kcal
Serving size: 1

Ingredients:

- 2 large eggs
- 30ml milk
- Salt
- Pepper
- 1 bacon slice

Preparation:

1. Break the eggs into a bowl and pour the milk into it.
2. Sprinkle some salt and pepper and whisk thoroughly.
3. Cook in the oven for a minute and stir again with a fork.
4. Cook for another 30 seconds till eggs are set but still a little runny.
5. Serve with a slice of baked bacon.

Salmon egg wrap

Cooked salmon served in an egg-wrap is an appetizing low-carb breakfast.

Net carbs: 2.7grams
Proteins: 27.5grams
Fats: 15.9grams
Calories: 261kcal
Serving size: 1

Ingredients:

- 2 large whisked eggs
- 1 tbsp chopped chives
- Salt
- Pepper
- 1 tbsp olive oil
- 2 tbsp Greek yogurt
- 1 tbsp lime juice and zest
- 40 grams smoked salmon cut into strips
- 1 cup spinach, watercress, and rocket leaf salad

Preparation:

1. Combine eggs with herbs, salt, and pepper.
2. Add a tsp of oil in a pan and pour the egg mixture on it.
3. Flip sides to cook the egg on both sides. Set aside.
4. Mix the lemon juice, zest, yogurt, and pepper in a bowl.
5. Adjust the salmon pieces on the egg wrap.
6. Add plenty of salad and a drizzle of the yogurt-lime mixture.
7. Roll the egg wrap and serve.

Chapter 12: Low-carb Vegetable Recipes

Greek salad

A plate full of low-carb veggies and feta makes a healthy and nice salad.

Net carbs: 13.9grams
Proteins: 10.1grams
Fats: 14.3grams
Calories: 261kcal
Serving size: 4
Ingredients:

- 2 sliced tomatoes
- 1 sliced cucumber
- 1 sliced onion
- 1 sliced green pepper
- 16 olives with pts removed
- 8 ounces crumbled feta
- 1 tsp oregano
- Olive oil

Preparation:

1. Assemble the veggies in a large bowl and drizzle some olive oil on it.
2. Toss to combine.
3. Sprinkle some oregano and top with the crumbled feta and serve.

Eggplant Parmesan boats

Eggplants stuffed with lots of cheese makes a mouth-watering dinner or lunch.

Net carbs: 24grams
Proteins: 20grams
Fats: 29grams
Calories: 442kcal
Serving size: 4

Ingredients:

- 2 eggplants
- 1/2 tsp olive oil
- 1 diced onion
- 2 chopped garlic cloves
- 2 cups marinara sauce
- Salt
- Pepper
- 1 cup shredded mozzarella
- 1/4 cup grated Parmesan

Preparation:

1. Cut eggplant lengthwise and scoop out the flesh. Reserve it.
2. Coat the eggplant boats with oil and roast at 400F for 15 minutes. set aside.
3. Sauté onion, reserved eggplant, and garlic in a pan for 8-10 minutes.
4. Add marinara sauce, salt, and pepper and cook on low flame for 5 minutes.
5. Fill the eggplant boats with the acquired sauce mixture and top with cheese.
6. Bake for 15 minutes and serve.

Low-carb Mexican casserole

Different kinds of peppers cooked with cauliflower rice and cheese is an amazing lunch delicacy.

Net carbs: 4.5grams

Proteins: 4.6grams

Fats: 10grams

Calories: 70kcal

Serving size: 12

Ingredients:

- 1 bowl cauliflower florets
- 1/2 onion
- 1 diced red bell pepper, green bell pepper, and jalapeno
- 1 tsp cumin
- 8 halved cherry tomatoes
- 1-1/2 cups cheese

Preparation:

1. Preheat the oven to 350F.
2. Sauté onions in some oil till soft and add peppers and cumin.
3. Grind the cauliflower florets into a fine rice and bake for a minute.
4. Mix it with the cherry tomatoes and cheese. Set aside.
5. Combine the cauliflower mixture with the pepper mix.
6. Spread the acquired mixture on an oil-coated baking dish and bake for 30 minutes. Serve.

Kale-stuffed Portobello mushrooms

Portobello mushrooms stuffed with cheese and kale is an ideal low-carb side dish.

Net carbs: 11.6grams

Proteins: 21.6grams

Fats: 21.9grams

Calories: 318kcal

Serving size: 4

Ingredients:

- 8 large Portobello mushrooms
- 6 oz kale
- 8 cheese slices
- 2 tbsp olive oil

Preparation:

1. Preheat the oven to 375F.
2. Place the mushrooms upside down in a baking dish and drizzle some oil on each.
3. Bake for 10 minutes and top with a cheese slice and kale.
4. Bake each mushroom for another 3 minutes till cheese melts. Serve.

Spinach and feta pie

This dish contains plenty of cheese and spinach. It is a great option for lunch.

Net carbs: 4.2grams
Proteins: 10.6grams
Fats: 16grams
Calories: 209kcal
Serving size: 12

Ingredients:

Pie crust:

- 150 grams almond flour
- 1 egg
- 1 tbsp coconut flour
- Salt
- Pepper

Spinach and feta pie filling

- 500 grams spinach
- 6 whisked eggs
- 1/2 diced onion
- 250 grams crumbled cheese and full-fat cheese
- Chopped mint
- Salt
- Pepper

Preparation:

Pie crust

1. Combine all the pie crust ingredients.
2. Coat a baking dish with some oil and spread the pie crust evenly in it.
3. Poke holes all over the crust with a fork and bake at 350F for 15 minutes. Set aside.

Spinach and feta pie filling

1. Drain all the water from the spinach and transfer it to a bowl with all other ingredients.
2. Combine everything but keep some cheese lumps intact.
3. Spoon out on the pie crust and bake at 350F for 40 minutes. Serve.

Stuffed baby peppers

Cheese stuffed baby peppers make a good low-carb side dish. Go for it.
Net carbs: 2.2grams
Proteins: 7.1grams
Fats: 13.9grams
Calories: 201kcal
Serving size: 2
Ingredients:
● 2 seeded baby peppers
● 1-1/2 cup cream cheese
● 1 tbsp mixed herbs
Preparation:
1. Sprinkle a tbsp of mixed herbs on the cream cheese and mix thoroughly.
2. Stuff each seeded bell pepper with the cream cheese mix with the help of a butter knife.
3. Bake for 3 minutes till cheese melts and peppers turn tender. Serve.

Spiralized zucchini Asian salad

Zucchini with almonds and seeds is a good low-carb option. Include it in your menu as a salad.
Net carbs: 4.1grams
Proteins: 4grams
Fats: 6.3grams
Calories: 120kcal
Serving size: 10
Ingredients:
● 1 spiralized zucchini
● 1 pound shredded cabbage
● 1 cup shelled sunflower seeds
● 1 cup sliced almonds
● 1/3 cup vinegar
● 1 tsp Stevia
Preparation:
1. Chop the zucchini in small pieces.
2. Assemble cabbage, sunflower seeds, and almonds in a bowl and add zucchini to it.
3. Take another bowl and mix oil, vinegar, and Stevia in it.
4. Pour the dressing on the salad and refrigerate for some time. Serve.

Spinach mushroom cheese quiche

Mushrooms, cheese, and spinach cooked with eggs is a satisfying low-carb delicacy that you should try.

Net carbs: 2.2grams
Proteins: 12grams
Fats: 14.9grams
Calories: 199kcal
Serving size: 6

Ingredients:

- 10 ounce thawed frozen spinach
- 4 ounce mushrooms
- 2 cheese slices
- 6 eggs
- 1/2 cup heavy cream and water
- 1/3 cup shredded Parmesan cheese
- 1/2 tsp garlic powder
- Salt
- Pepper
- 1 cup shredded mozzarella

Preparation:

1. Drain off the water from the spinach, spread it on a greased pie pan, and top it with mushrooms.
2. Crumble the cheese and spread over the mushrooms.
3. Beat the eggs thoroughly with water and cream. Stir in the Parmesan, garlic, salt, and pepper.
4. Pour the acquired mixture on the top of other pie pan ingredients.
5. Top with some mozzarella cheese and bake for 40 minutes at 350F. Serve.

Creamed Leeks

Leeks cooked in butter and cheese is yummy to taste.
Net carbs: 3.1grams
Proteins: 1.2grams
Fats: 8.4grams
Calories: 105kcal
Serving size: 4
Ingredients:
- 2 sliced leeks
- 2 tbsp butter
- 2 minced garlic cloves
- 25 grams cream cheese
- Pepper

Preparation:
1. Melt the butter in a pan and cook garlic in it.
2. Add leeks and cook till tender.
3. Add a dash of salt and pepper and stir well before serving.

Avocado salsa

Avocado chunks mixed with chili, onion, and tomato is a savory low-carb side dish that you can add in your menu.
Net carbs: 5.3grams
Proteins: 2grams
Fats: 14grams
Calories: 178kcal
Serving size: 8
Ingredients:
- 4 avocados
- 1 lemon
- 1/2 cup heavy cream
- 1 diced chili, onion, and tomato

Preparation:
1. Peel the avocados and cut into slices.
2. Place in a bowl and add rest of the ingredients.
3. Combine everything well but let the avocado chunk remain. Serve.

Chapter 13-Low-carb snacks and desserts

Low-carb crunchy snacks

Crispy Parmesan chips

Parmesan cheese baked into chips is a great low-carb munch.

Net carbs: 2grams

Proteins: 2grams

Fats: 9grams

Calories: 69kcal

Serving size: 15

Ingredients:

- 30 wonton wrappers
- Cooking spray
- 2 tbsp olive oil
- 1 minced garlic clove
- 1/2 tsp dried basil
- 1/4 cup grated Parmesan cheese

Preparation:

1. Preheat oven to 350F.
2. Slice the wonton wrappers in half to make 60 triangles.
3. Spray some cooking spray on a non-stick pan and arrange the triangles on it.
4. Mix oil, garlic, and basil in a bowl and brush the triangles with it.
5. Top with the crumbled cheese and bake for 8 minutes till crispy. Serve.

Mixed nuts crunch

Different nuts baked in butter and spice is a nice low-carb evening munch.

Net carbs: 3grams
Proteins: 2grams
Fats: 12grams
Calories: 82kcal
Serving size: 20

Ingredients:

- 4 cups mixed cashews, walnuts, pistachios, and other nuts
- 1 cup coconut flour
- 1/2 cup sliced almonds
- 2 tbsp molten butter
- 1/2 tsp apple pie spice
- Salt

Preparation:

1. Combine all the nuts in a bowl and add molten butter, apple pie spice, and salt to it.
2. Pour the mixture over the coconut flour and combine well.
3. Make small balls from the mixture and bake for 20 minutes till almonds are toasted. Let the balls cool and serve.

Walnut raspberry thumbprints

Walnut cookies with raspberry syrup topping is a great low-carb evening snack.

Net carbs: 0.4grams
Proteins: 1gram
Fats: 6grams
Calories: 61kcal
Serving size: 40

Ingredients:

- 1/4 cup molten butter
- 1 tbsp Stevia
- 1/2 tsp baking powder
- 1/4 tsp cardamom powder
- 1/8 tsp baking soda
- 2 egg whites
- 1/2 tsp vanilla essence
- 1 cup almond flour
- 1 whisked egg
- 4 tbsp chopped walnuts
- 1/4 cup raspberry syrup

Preparation:

1. Combine all the ingredients except whisked egg and raspberry syrup in a blender and make a fine dough.
2. Refrigerate the dough for 2 hours.
3. Preheat oven to 375F.
4. Make small balls from the dough and dip each ball in the whisked egg.
5. Arrange on a baking sheet and make a deep groove in each ball.
6. Bake for 8 minutes till cookies turn brown.
7. Let the cookies cool and add a spoonful of raspberry syrup into each indentation. Serve.

Yo-yos

Yo-yos are low-carb wafers coated with dark chocolate and strawberry syrup.

Net carbs: 0.3grams
Proteins: 4grams
Fats: 5grams
Calories: 73kcal
Serving size: 12
Ingredients:
- 1/4 cup 100% dark chocolate chips
- 1/2 tsp shortening
- 24 vanillawafers
- 1/2 cup strawberry syrup(unsweetened)

Preparation:
1. Melt chocolate chips and shortening in a pan and apply the mixture on the flat side of each wafer and let it set.
2. Drop a spoonful of strawberry syrup on top of the chocolate and cover with another wafer.
3. Set in the freezer for 4hours and serve.

Low-carb delicious desserts

Strawberry peanut butter smoothie

Smoothie made from strawberries and butter is a refreshing low-carb dessert.

Net carbs: 2.4grams
Proteins: 13grams
Fats: 21grams
Calories: 118kcal
Serving size: 1
Ingredients:
- 1 cup sliced strawberries
- 1 cup coconut milk
- Ice cubes
- 2 tbsp molten peanut butter
- 1 bowl heavy whipping cream

Preparation:
1. Throw all the ingredients in a blender and pulse into a thick smoothie.
2. Pour the smoothie in a glass bowl and serve with a few strawberry slices.

Cashew butter jelly

Cashew paste layered with berry syrup is a yummy low-carb dessert.

Net carbs: 4.2grams   **Fats: 10grams**

Proteins: 7.1grams   **Calories: 109kcal**

Serving size: 3

Ingredients:

- 2 cups cashews
- A dash of salt
- 1 tbsp oil
- 3 drops of liquid Stevia
- 1 cup homemade mixed berries sugar-free jelly

Preparation:

1. Grind the cashews, salt, and oil into a granular powder.
2. Drop a few Stevia drops into the powder and a few tbsp of milk till a fine paste is formed.
3. Take a glass jar and arrange the acquired batter and jelly layer by layer.
4. Set in the fridge for some time before serving.

Blueberry cheesecake

It is a mouth-watering dessert made from blueberries, almond flour, and cream cheese.

Net carbs: 7.2grams   **Fats: 31grams**

Proteins: 18grams   **Calories: 241kcal**

Serving size: 8

Ingredients:

- 1/2 cup full-fat cream cheese
- 2 tbsp Greek yogurt
- 2 tsp lime juice and blueberry preserves
- 1 cup diced blueberries
- 1/2 cup almond powder
- Few drops of Stevia

Preparation:

1. Mix thoroughly the cream cheese, yogurt, lime juice and Stevia in a bowl and refrigerate for some time.
2. Combine preserves and blueberries in a separate bowl.
3. Mix the almond flour with a little Stevia and set aside.
4. Arrange the three mixtures layer after layer in 8 glasses and refrigerate. Serve.

Dark chocolate muffins

Give this low-carb dessert made from dark chocolate and coconut flour a try. It tastes yummy.

Net carbs: 5.3grams
Proteins: 15grams
Fats: 27grams
Calories: 258kcal
Serving size: 1

Ingredients:

- 1 cup 100% dark chocolate chips
- 1 cup butter and coconut flour
- 1 cup unsweetened vanilla extract

Preparation:

1. Preheat the oven to 350C.
2. Melt the chocolate chips and butter in a pan and add vanilla essence and coconut flour to it.
3. Combine into a fine batter.
4. Spray few muffin molds with cooking spray and spoon out the batter into each mold.
5. Bake for 10 minutes till the muffins are done.
6. Let the muffins cool before serving.

Chapter 14 – Low-carb soups and stews
Low-carb soup recipes
Chicken salsa soup
Chicken breasts cooked in broth and other low-carb ingredients make a great soup.

Calories: 92 kcal
Proteins: 10.6grams
Total carbs: 9.5grams
Fat: 1.13grams
Servings: 1
Ingredients:
- 1/2 lb chicken breast
- 14-1/2 Oz chicken broth
- 14-1/2 oz water
- 2 tsp chili powder
- 1 cup corn
- 8 oz salsa
- 1 cup chopped carrots

Preparation:
1. In a pan, combine chicken, broth, water, and chili powder and boil.
2. Reduce heat, cover and simmer for 5 minutes.
3. Add corn and carrots and return to boil.
4. Cook till chicken and corn turns tender and add salsa.
5. Garnish with cheese and serve.

Mixed veggie soup

Plenty of veggies cooked in chicken stock with herbs is a nice low-carb soup recipe.

Calories: 58 kcal
Proteins: 2.8grams
Total carbs: 10.1grams
Fat: 1.04grams
Servings: 1

Ingredients:
- 1 head cabbage
- 1 lb onion
- 2 cups chopped bell pepper, celery
- 5 cloves garlic
- 4 cups chopped carrots
- 1 packet onion soup mix
- Salt
- Pepper
- 1 tbsp garlic
- 6 cups chicken broth
- 4 cups, pieces, and slices of mushroom
- 1 tbsp oil

Preparation:
1. Heat oil and fry onions, garlic and pepper in it.
2. Add celery, carrots, soup mix and mushrooms and boil.
3. Turn down to simmer and then add cabbage and water until cabbage is covered.
4. Cook for one hour and serve.

Celery, onion and spinach soup

This soup is made from veggies and chicken bouillon cubes. It tastes yummy.

Calories: 43 kcal

Proteins: 3.1grams

Total carbs: 7.8grams

Fat: 0.6grams

Servings: 1

Ingredients:

● 10 oz frozen onion, spinach

● 6 stalks large celery

● 4 cubes chicken bouillon

● 4 cups water

Preparation:

1. In a pan put 4 bouillon cubes of chicken with 4 cups water.
2. Allow it to boil and add frozen vegetables and celery.
3. Stir it occasionally so that bouillon separates and vegetables get mixed and flavors seep.
4. Boil it for another 5 minutes and then simmer for 10-15 minutes.
5. Add pepper and enjoy.

Egg drop soup

Eggs and mixed veggies boiled in chicken stock is a perfect low-carb soup recipe.

Calories: 83 kcal

Proteins: 6.5grams

Total carbs: 4.9grams

Fat: 4.08grams

Servings: 1

Ingredients:

● 3 eggs, lightly beaten
● 4 cups chicken stock
● 1 tbsp cornstarch
● 1/2 tsp grated ginger
● 1 tbsp soya sauce
● 3 stalks chopped green onion
● 1/4 tsp white pepper
● 3/4 piecesmushrooms

Preparation:

1. Mix cornstarch in stock and stir until dissolved.
2. Place chicken stock, ginger, soy sauce, green onions, mushrooms and white pepper in a pan and boil.
3. Stir in the cornstarch mixture and reduce the heat.
4. Slowly pour the beaten eggs while stirring the top.
5. Garnish with chopped green onions and serve.

Delicious low-carb stews

Low-carb beef stew

Beef stew is not only yummy to taste but very health too. It contains plenty of low-carb ingredients.

Calories: 288 kcal
Proteins: 20grams
Total carbs: 4grams
Fat: 20grams
Servings: 6
Ingredients:

- 1-1/4 pound cubed beef chuck roasted
- 8 ounces quartered mushrooms
- 6 ounces peeled celery roots
- 4 ounces peeled onions
- 3 sliced celery ribs
- 2 minced garlic cloves
- 2 tbsp tomato paste
- 5 tbsp olive oil
- 5 cups beef broth
- 1 bay leaf
- 1/2 tsp dried thyme
- Salt
- Pepper

Preparation:

1. Add mushrooms to oil-coated large cooking pot and cook for 2 minutes and remove.
2. Cook beef till brown and add bay leaf, spices, salt, pepper, and tomato paste.
3. Pour the broth into the pot and set on low-flame for 1-1/2 hours.
4. Add veggies and cook for another 40 minutes till meat and veggies are soft. Serve.

Lamb instant pot stew

Lamb meat cooked in an instant pot with many other ingredients makes a mouth-watering stew.

Calories: 462kcal
Proteins: 30grams
Total carbs: 2.2grams
Fat: 37grams
Servings: 15
Ingredients:
- 1/2 cup tallow and vinegar
- 3 garlic cloves, minced
- 1 slicedonion
- 1/2 cup rosemary
- 3 chopped celery sticks
- Salt
- Pepper
- 1cup tomato puree
- 4cups beef broth
- 4pounds lamb bones
- 1/2 pound stemmed mushrooms

Preparation:
1. Put tallow, garlic, onion, celery, and rosemary leaves in an instant pot and select the sauté mode.
2. Add rest of the ingredients and cook on stew mode for 5hours.
3. Remove all the meat from the bones before discarding.
4. Now add the mushrooms and reduce the gravy to half. Serve.

Delicious low-carb seafood stew

Seafood boiled in chicken stock and other ingredients is a very heath soup recipe.

Calories: 411kcal

Proteins: 31grams

Total carbs: 6.1grams

Fat: 46grams

Servings: 4

Ingredients:

- 1 lb white fish pieces
- 12 shrimps-washed and peeled
- 1 cup prawn meat
- 1 sliced onion
- 2 garlic cloves
- 1peeled and chopped radish
- 2 cups chicken stock
- 1-1/2 cup almond milk
- 2 tbsp coconut oil
- Salt
- Pepper

Preparation:

1. Pour some coconut oil in a pan and cook shrimp. Set aside.
2. Add spices and radish to the same pot and cook for 5 minutes.
3. Now add all the meat and chicken stock and let the contents boil.
4. Transfer the shrimp back to the pot and cook for 15 minutes.
5. Pour the almond milk and serve.

Vinegar herbs and chicken stew

Chicken boiled in chicken stock with herbs and vinegar makes a great low-carb stew.

Calories: 256 kcal

Proteins: 10grams

Total carbs: 2.8grams

Fat: 15grams

Servings: 6

Ingredients:

- 10 cups chicken stock
- 3 tbsp olive oil
- 8 garlic cloves
- 1 sliced onion
- 1 cup white vinegar
- 2 boneless chicken breasts
- 1 tbsp mixed herbs
- 2 ounces crumbled cheese

Preparation:

1. Cook onion and garlic in a pot till it turns soft.
2. Add chicken and remaining ingredients except for cheese and bring the contents to boil. Cook for 20 minutes.
3. Shred the tender chicken breasts and top with some crumbled cheese. Serve.

Chapter 15-Low-carb appetizers
Low- carb hot appetizers
Cheesy sausage stuffed mushrooms

Mushrooms stuffed with cream and sausage is a nice low-carb starter.

Calories: 192kcal

Proteins: 7.8 grams

Total carbs: 4.3grams

Fat: 16.5grams

Servings: 12

Ingredients:

- 3-8 ounces mushrooms, clean and stem removed
- 12 ounces pork sausage
- 1 tsp garlic, basil, parsley
- 2-3 tsp chili pepper
- 8 ounces softened cream cheese

Preparation:

1. Preheat oven to 350F.
2. Scoop inside of mushroom to make room for filling and place it in a baking dish.
3. Put sausage in a skillet and fry it till brown, add pastes and stir it.
4. Place the cream cheese in a mixer and add to your sausage, blend it.
5. Stuff each mushroom with the mixture and bake for 30 minutes.
6. Remove and sprinkle chili pepper and parsley.
7. Put mushrooms on a serving plate and enjoy.

Mini bun-less cheeseburger bites with thousand island dip

This low-carb starter is made of plenty of ingredients including beef, bacon, and yogurt. Give it a try.

Calories: 236kcal
Proteins: 20.1 grams
Total carbs: 1.7grams
Fat: 16.3grams
Servings: 16

Ingredients:

- 2 pounds beef
- Salt and pepper
- 1/2 tsp onion powder
- 1 tsp garlic powder
- 6 ounces bacon
- 24 cherry tomatoes halved
- 2 cups red leaf chopped lettuce
- 8 ounces cheddar cheese.

Thousand island dip:

- 1 clove garlic minced
- 1 cup plain Greek yogurt
- 1 tbsp olive oil
- 2 tbsp sugar-free ketchup
- Salt and pepper

Preparation:

1. Preheat oven to 400 degrees.
2. Mix the first 5 ingredients in a bowl.
3. Using 1 tbsp of meat mixture, make 48 mini meatballs.
4. Place them on a baking sheet and bake for 15 minutes.
5. Cook the bacon in a skillet, remove and break into 48 pieces.
6. To make a burger on toothpick start with a tomato half, bacon, lettuce, cheese, and burger.

Cheddar cheese straws

This delicious appetizer is made of cheese, coconut flour, and other ingredients. It is a great starter option.

Calories: 163kcal

Proteins: 5 grams

Total carbs: 5grams

Fat: 14grams

Servings: 24

Ingredients:

- 1 cup almond flour
- 2 tbsp coconut flour and arrow starch
- 1 tbsp xanthan gum
- 1/2 tsp garlic powder
- Salt
- 5 tbsp butter
- 2-4 tbsp ice water
- 4 Oz finely shredded cheddar

Preparation:

1. Mix almond flour, coconut flour, arrowroot starch, xanthan gum, garlic powder and salt in a food processor.
2. Sprinkle butter over the above mixture and pulse until it resembles fine crumbs.
3. Put it into a flat disc, cover with plastic wrap and chill for 30 minutes.
4. Preheat oven to 300f and line it with baking sheet.
5. Take 1 tbsp of dough and roll it between the palms into a cigar shape.
6. Sprinkle it with grated cheese and bake it for 25 minutes, until firm and cheese becomes lightly brown.
7. Remove from the oven and let cool completely.

Grain-free spinach crackers

This is a perfect light and yummy starter recipe.

Calories: 126kcal

Proteins: 4.5grams

Total carbs: 4.2grams

Fat: 10.9grams

Servings: 24

Ingredients:

- 150g fresh thawed spinach
- 1-1/2 cup almond flour
- 1/4 cup coconut flour
- 1/2 cup flax meal
- 1/4 cup butter or ghee
- 1/2 tsp ground cumin
- 1/2 tsp dried, flaked chili peppers
- 1/2 grated parmesan cheese
- salt

Preparation:

1. Boil spinach in water till wilted.
2. Squeeze the water and blend until smooth.
3. Mix all other ingredients including spinach into the dough.
4. Wrap in a foil and refrigerate for an hour.
5. Preheat oven to 200C.
6. Roll the dough into 1/2cm thickness. Slice and bake for 20minutes.

Low- carb cold appetizers

Cucumber cream cheese sandwiches

Grated cucumber served with cheese makes a great starter.

Calories: 47kcal
Proteins: 3grams
Total carbs: 2grams
Fat: 2grams
Servings: 20

Ingredients:

- 3 Oz cream cheese
- 1 medium cucumber
- 1 tbsp sour cream
- Dash of salt, pepper and garlic powder
- Low-carb bread

Preparation:

1. Wash, clean and grate the cucumber and drain away the liquid.
2. Mix the cream cheese, cucumber, sour cream until smooth. Season with salt, pepper and garlic powder.
3. Spread cucumber mixture on one bread slice and cover with top slice, cut in half and serve.

White cheddar cucumber chips

Cucumber tossed with mixed spices is a known low-carb starter.

Calories: 127kcal
Proteins: 5.3grams
Total carbs: 4.5grams
Fat: 10.9grams
Servings: 6

Ingredients:

- 6 cups sliced cucumber
- 2 tbsp olive oil
- Dash of salt, pepper, onion powder and garlic powder
- 1/2 cup grated white cheddar cheese

Preparation:

1. Toss the sliced cucumber with oil and keep aside.
2. Mix the seasoning in a bowl.
3. Put the cucumber slices on the dehydrator and be sure they are coated well with oil.
4. Sprinkle the seasoning on all the slices and put the grated cheese over them.
5. Allow dehydrating for 8-10 hours.

Greek avocado and feta cucumber cups

Cucumber, cheese, and avocados together make an amazing low-carb appetizer.

Calories: 39kcal
Proteins: 1grams
Total carbs: 3grams
Fat: 13grams
Servings: 1

Ingredients:

- 1 cucumber cut crosswise into 1-inch piece
- 1 avocado peeled and pitted
- 1 tsp lemon juice
- 1/2 tomato, diced
- 2 tbsp crumbled feta cheese
- 3 pitted olives, sliced
- Salt and pepper
- Parsley for garnish

Preparation:

1. Remove the flesh of a cucumber piece, leaving the bottom intact.
2. Mash the avocado and stir in lemon juice, tomato, feta cheese, olives, salt, and pepper.
3. Fill each cucumber cup with the above mixture. Garnish it with parsley and serve.

Salt and vinegar zucchini chips

Baked zucchini slice with vinegar is a low-carb appetizer relished by all.

Calories: 40kcal

Proteins: 0.7grams

Total carbs: 2.9grams

Fat: 3.6grams

Servings: 8

Ingredients:

● 4 cups thinly sliced zucchini

● 2 tbsp olive oil

● 2 tbsp white balsamic vinegar

● Salt

Preparation:

1. Whisk oil, salt, and vinegar in a bowl and toss with the zucchini.
2. Preheat oven to 200F and line it with baking sheet. Lay the zucchini evenly on it and bake for 2.5 hours.
3. Allow it to cool and store chips in an airtight container.

Chapter 16 – Low-carb drinks

White chocolate peppermint mocha

This is a refreshing low-carb energy-packed drink.

Calories: 320 kcal

Proteins: 2 grams

Total carbs: 3grams

Fat: 34grams

Servings: 1

Ingredients:

- 6 Oz almond milk
- 1 shot espresso
- 1 tbsp powdered erythritol
- 1/2 tsp vanilla extract
- 1 Oz cocoa butter
- 1 scoop hot cocoa
- Whipped cream
- Drops of peppermint extract

Preparation:

1. Heat milk in a pan until steamy.
2. Add a a shot of espresso, erythritol, vanilla extract, and cocoa butter. Remove from the heat and stir until the cocoa butter is fully melted.
3. Add a scoop of hot cocoa and whisk until fully incorporated.
4. Pour it in a mug and top it with cream and few drops of peppermint extract.

Browned butter pumpkin spice latte

Pumpkin spice latte is a very healthy high-fat, low-carb drink.

Calories: 235 kcal

Proteins:1grams

Total carbs: 7grams

Fat: 23grams

Servings: 1

Ingredients:

- 1 tbsp butter
- 1 shot espresso
- 2 tbsp erythritol, pumpkin puree
- 2 tbsp heavy cream
- 1/4 tsp pumpkin pie spice
- 1/2 tsp cinnamon
- Salt
- 1/2 cup almond milk

Preparation:

1. Melt butter in a pan. Put a shot of espresso.
2. Combine erythritol and hot coffee in a blender and allow dissolving, lightly whisk.
3. Add pumpkin puree, butter, heavy cream, pumpkin pie spice, cinnamon, and salt. Then put almond milk to make mixture thin.
4. Blend the mixture for 10 seconds.
5. Pour into a serving cup and top with cream and sprinkle of cinnamon and enjoy!

Keto hot cocoa

Almond milk with hot cocoa and heavy cream is nothing short of a perfect low-carb drink.

Calories: 173 kcal
Proteins:2grams
Total carbs: 4grams
Fat: 15grams
Servings: 1
Ingredients:
- 6 Oz almond milk
- 1 scoop hot cocoa
- 2 tbsp heavy cream
- 3-6 drops stevia
- Whipped cream
- Chocolate Shavings

Preparation:
1. Heat milk, add a scoop of hot cocoa and heavy cream and whisk until completely dissolved.
2. Top with whipped cream and chocolate shavings.

Thai iced tea

It is a low-carb brew that is very refreshing and yummy.

Calories: 200 kcal
Proteins:1grams
Total carbs: 5grams
Fat: 20grams
Servings: 1
Ingredients:
- 1 bag Thai tea
- 1/2 cup boiling water
- 6-8 ice cubes
- 1/4 heavy cream
- 8 drops stevia

Preparation:
1. Steep a bag of tea in boiling water for 5 minutes.
2. Remove the tea bag and put tea into a serving glass with 6-8 ice cubes.
3. Pour heavy cream and Stevia and stir it till combined.
4. Enjoy.

Keto Mojito

Keto Mojio is a drink that refreshes and energizes you. It is low in carbs and tastes great.

Calories: 140 kcal

Proteins:0grams

Total carbs: 4grams

Fat: 0grams

Servings: 1

Ingredients:

- 10 large mint leaves
- 1 Oz fresh lime juice
- 1 tsp powdered erythritol
- 1 cup ice cubes
- 2 Oz white rum and club soda

Preparation:

1. Put mint leaves in a glass, add lime juice, erythritol and ice cubes.
2. Pour white rum and club soda and stir to mix everything.
3. Garnish it with mint leaves.

Fruit infused iced tea

Fruit flavored ice tea is a favorite drink of many low-carb dieter. Give it a try.

Calories: 100kcal
Proteins:0grams
Total carbs: 3grams
Fat: 0grams
Servings: 1

Ingredients:

- 2 cups boiled water
- 1 tea bag
- 1 strawberry
- 1 slice lemon
- Stevia
- 1 tbsp vinegar
- Ice

Preparation:

1. Put a pot of water to boil and once boiled begin brewing your tea.
2. Cut a strawberry into pieces and add it along a slice of lemon into the tea.
3. Add ice and Stevia to your glass.
4. Pour the brewed tea into the glass submerging the fruit and stir it.
5. Top it up with apple cider vinegar.

With this, I end the recipes section of this book. The tastes are vast, flavors are magical, and choices are innumerable. All you need to do is try new things and expand your menu. If you do so, trust me dear readers, the low-carb journey will be the most effective and delicious diet plan you can ever take.

CPSIA information can be obtained
at www.ICGtesting.com
Printed in the USA
LVHW061357290521
688880LV00003B/358

9 781649 845313